hologram

HOLOGRAM

A BOOK OF GLOSAS

P K PAGE

Brick Books

CANADIAN CATALOGUING IN PUBLICATION DATA

Page, P.K. (Patricia Kathleen), 1916-
  Hologram: a book of glosas

Poems.
ISBN 0-919626-72-6

I. Title.

PS8531.A44H6 1994   C811'.54   C94-931416-1
PR9199.3.P34H6 1994

The support of the Canada Council and the Ontario Arts
Council is gratefully acknowledged. The support of the
Government of Ontario through the Ministry of Culture,
Tourism and Recreation is also gratefully acknowledged.

The cover painting is 'Votive Tablet' by P.K. Irwin.
Reproduced by courtesy of Mike Doyle.

Page decorations are by P.K. Irwin.

Calligraphy is by Théa Gray.

The four lines that appear at the beginning of 'Hologram',
'Autumn', 'Planet Earth' were translated respectively by Rex
Warner, Stephen Mitchell, and Alastair Reid. The four lines
that appear at the beginning of 'Alone' are Fragment 125,
translator unknown.

Brick Books
431 Boler Road, Box 20081
London, Ontario N6K 4G6

for Arthur
as always

for Florence and Jori
old friends

and Théa
new

CONTENTS

I was introduced to the glosa through the ear. Its form, half hidden, powerfully sensed, like an iceberg at night, made me search for its outline as I listened. The eye, of course, sees it at a glance: the opening quatrain written by another poet; followed by four ten-line stanzas, their concluding lines taken consecutively from the quatrain; their sixth and ninth lines rhyming with the borrowed tenth. Used by the poets of the Spanish court, the form dates back to the late 14th and early 15th century. It has not been popular in English.

For some reason I found it challenging – rather in the way a crossword puzzle is challenging. I picked up the first book of poems that came to hand – Seferis, as it happened – in search of four suitable lines. As is often the case at the moment of challenge, everything was easy. Beginner's luck, they call it. Almost without trying, I found the lines that launched 'Hologram'. I won't say I wrote it in a flash, but in a near-flash. The words that controlled the rhymes were *angle, sea, peacock,* and *it.* It was immediately clear that full rhymes would be difficult. Any rhymester knows that English is not Spanish.

I enjoyed the idea of constructing the poem backwards – the final line of each stanza is, in effect, the starting line. You work towards a known. I liked being controlled by those three reining rhymes – or do I mean reigning? – and gently influenced by the rhythm of the original. I felt as if I were hand in hand with Seferis. A curious marriage – two sensibilities intermingling. Little did I then know how obsessed I would become by the form and how, as with all obsessions, it would have to run its course. And little did I know what hazards would lie ahead.

Having completed 'Hologram' relatively easily, it occurred to me that now, towards the end of my life, it would be appropriate to use this form as a way of paying homage to those poets

whose work I fell in love with in my formative years. I would
pick four lines from Marvell, Blake, Donne, Yeats, Lorca, Rilke,
Hopkins, Auden and Eliot and, as it were, 'marry' them. And so
I retraced the steps of my early reading – but this time with a
different intention. It was a wonderful journey. And full of
surprises. I had had so little difficulty with Seferis, it never
occurred to me I would run into problems with anyone else. But
I soon discovered that border raids were not necessarily going to
be easy. Read as I might, I could not find four consecutive lines
in Marvell, Blake, Donne, Yeats, Lorca or Hopkins that would
'marry' me.

At first I had no clear understanding of what I needed from the
borrowed lines – gradually I learned. They had to be end-
stopped, or give the illusion of so being; as nine of my lines
would separate them from each other, they had to give me nine
lines' worth of space; as well, their rhythm had to be one I
could work with, *not* from the level at which one does an
exercise – one can do anything as an exercise – but from that
deeper level where one's own drums beat. Finally, and vitally,
they had to parallel in an intimate way my own knowledge,
experience, or – but preferably and – some other indefinable
factor I could recognize but not name. Anyone who has ever
attempted to match fabrics will know what I mean – it is not
colour alone or texture or weight, but all of them in
combination. Frequently four lines would meet one
requirement but not the others.

For my second glosa, 'The Gold Sun', I borrowed lines from
Wallace Stevens. They were not enjambed, I was comfortable
with their rhythm and, as an additional benefit, the rhyming
words were reasonably easy. But I was drawn to them especially
because they offered me an opposite view from the one
expressed in 'A Little Reality', the second section of my poem,

'Kaleidoscope'. Even as I wrote it I knew that Reality is glimpsed not only by addition – courtesy of 'the perfect, all-inclusive metaphor' – but by subtraction as well. Stevens' lines offered me a poem of subtraction – a kind of negative-space companion poem. Would I have thought of it on my own? I wonder.

It was some time before I was able to write a third glosa. I searched through Rilke, often so caught up in his poetry that I forgot the purpose of my reading. When I did remember, I was frustrated by page after page of wonderful enjambed verse. At last, in Stephen Mitchell's translation of 'Autumn Day' I found what I needed. Rilke had been one of the overwhelming poets of my youth. His *Duino Elegies* had frequently accompanied me on my way to work by streetcar in Montreal and, more than once, totally engrossed in his images, I had ended up at the car barns. A book of homage would be incomplete if I could not include him.

The poets of my youth were almost all male. Although Marianne Moore had published a *Selected Poems* in 1935 I hadn't read her until much later. But it was unnecessary for me to open her books to know how unaccommodating her lines would be. To find what I needed I had to jump forward in time to Elizabeth Bishop.

I spent a long time on Akmatova, not yet translated when I was young, but a powerful poetic presence in my later life. Although most adults have suffered some kind of grief or loss, I knew as I read Akmatova with the intention of selecting four of her lines that the task I had set myself was impossible. How could I accompany her – even in a poem where I was, after all, free to invent?

The real work of writing the glosas proved to be this search for suitable lines. 'Work' is hardly the correct word to describe spending the better part of a year reading one's favourite poets, but it *was* time consuming. And once having found the four lines, I was not necessarily home free. The losses were almost as numerous as the gains. I began and failed with Lorca, Spender, Jimenez, Hopkins, cummings, MacEwan – for now I was searching beyond the limits I had originally set myself.

'Who were the poets who influenced you?' interviewers often ask and I have always resisted the idea – not that I think my voice so original, but because 'affinity with' seems closer to the truth than 'influenced by'. This year, reading again the giants of my youth, I could not help wondering what their effect on me had been. Had I been influenced by any of them? And if so, how?

Timing is interesting. I had barely formulated the questions before I found what may be their answer in a report by an ornithologist. Attempting to understand how song birds learn to sing, he brought them up in isolation. To his surprise, they produced a kind of a song – not species perfect – but recognizable. He then introduced them to the songs of a variety of birds *not* of their species and discovered they chose the notes and cadences that, combined with their own attempts, completed their species song. 'Of course!' I thought, 'that is what poets do. We have a song – of a kind. But it is not until we have heard many other songs that we are able to put together our own specific song.'

If the analogy holds, this book contains some – regrettably not all – of the many songs I heard when, falteringly, I was searching for my own voice.

March, 1994   *P.K. Page*

All that morning we looked at the citadel from every angle.
We began from the side in the shadow, where the sea,
Green without brilliance, – breast of a slain peacock,
Received us like time that has no break in it.

The King of Asine   *George Seferis*

It was astonishing, larger by far than we could imagine,
larger than sight itself but still we strained to see it.
It was Kafka's castle in a dream of wonder,
nightmare transmuted, black become golden,
buttresses disappearing in the cloud and azure:
a new geometry of interlocking octangles
and we, watching it, interlocked in a strange dimension –
that neither your heart nor mine could have invented –
of multiple images, complex as angels.
All that morning we looked at the citadel from every angle.

But that was later, after we had made the passage
from the faint light of morning star and pale moon
to unscrupulous noonday with its major chords –
battalions marching across an Escher landscape.
For us, at first, there was no hint of clarity,
no hint of anything that wasn't misty –
synaesthetic layers and lengths of space-time
leading us inward, downward, upward, as –
from all directions at once – observing closely,
we began from the side in the shadow and the sea.

Brave of us to begin in darkness. Or was it wisdom
that made us so prepare ourselves for that radiance
little by little? A Jurassic age must pass before even colour
could enter the scene – dawn's greys being so infinite
and infinitely subtle – transparencies, opacities.
And then we sensed it together – the tremulous foreshock
of what lay ahead: what could not be imagined,
possibly not even dreamed, a new range of experience.
And – unbelievably – what revealed itself as earthquake
was green, without brilliance, breast of a slain peacock.

But to the cones of our eyes that green was shining
and pierced us like a spear. (When joy is great enough
how distinguish it from pain?) And after the fugal greys
and the near-invisible shafts of no-colour that had stained us,
how could our eyes adjust to so full a spectrum?
And yet in a flash, from infra-red to ultra-violet,
we saw the hologram glittering above us
glistening in air we could suddenly enter like swallows
as the whole citadel, rainbowed, immediate,
received us like time that has no break in it.

THE GOLD SUN

Trace the gold sun about the whitened sky
Without evasion by a single metaphor.
Look at it in its essential barrenness
And say this, this is the centre that I seek.

Credences of Summer   *Wallace Stevens*

Sky whitened by a snow on which no swan
is visible, and no least feather falling
could possibly or impossibly be seen,
sky whitened like the blank page of a book,
no letters forming into words unless
written in paleness – a pallidity
faint as the little rising moons on nails –
and so, forgettable and so, forgot.
Blue eyes dark as lapis lazuli
trace the gold sun about the whitened sky.

You'll see the thing itself no matter what.
Though it may blind you, what else will suffice?
To smoke a glass or use a periscope
will give you other than the very thing,
or more, or elements too various.
So let the fabulous photographer
catch Phaeton in his lens and think he is
the thing itself, not knowing all the else
he is become. But you will see it clear
without evasion by a single metaphor.

How strip the sun of all comparisons?
That spinning coin – moving, yet at rest
in its outflinging course across the great
parabola of space – is Phoebus,
sovereign: heroic principle,
the heat and light of us. And gold – no less
a metaphor than sun – is not the least
less multiple and married. Therefore how
rid the gold sun of all its otherness?
Look at it in its essential barrenness.

Make a prime number of it, pure, and know
it indivisible and hold it so
in the white sky behind your lapis eyes.
Push aside everything that isn't sun
the way a sculptor works his stone,
the way a mystic masters the mystique
of making more by focussing on one
until at length, all images are gone
except the sun, the thing itself, deific,
and say this, this is the centre that I seek.

AUTUMN

Whoever has no house now will never have one.
Whoever is alone will stay alone
Will sit, read, write long letters through the evening
And wander on the boulevards, up and down ...

Autumn Day   *Rainer Maria Rilke*

Its stain is everywhere.
The sharpening air
of late afternoon
is now the colour of tea.
Once-glycerined green leaves
burned by a summer sun
are brittle and ochre.
Night enters day like a thief.
And children fear that the beautiful daylight has gone.
Whoever has no house now will never have one.

It is the best and the worst time.
Around a fire, everyone laughing,
brocaded curtains drawn,
nowhere – anywhere – is more safe than here.
The whole world is a cup
one could hold in one's hand like a stone
warmed by that same summer sun.
But the dead or the near dead
are now all knucklebone.
Whoever is alone will stay alone.

Nothing to do. Nothing to really do.
Toast and tea are nothing.
Kettle boils dry.
Shut the night out or let it in,
it is a cat on the wrong side of the door
whichever side it is on. A black thing
with its implacable face.
To avoid it you
will tell yourself you are something,
will sit, read, write long letters through the evening.

Even though there is bounty, a full harvest
that sharp sweetness in the tea-stained air
is reserved for those who have made a straw
fine as a hair to suck it through –
fine as a golden hair.
Wearing a smile or a frown
God's face is always there.
It is up to you
if you take your wintry restlessness into the town
and wander on the boulevards, up and down.

... looking for something, something, something.
Poor bird, he is obsessed!
The millions of grains are black, white, tan, and gray,
mixed with quartz grains, rose and amethyst.

Sandpiper   *Elizabeth Bishop*

From birth, from the first astonishing moment
when he pecked his way out of the shell, pure fluff,
he was looking for something – warmth, food, love
or light, or darkness – we are all the same stuff,
all have the same needs: to be one of the flock
or to stand apart, a singular fledgling.
So the search began – the endless search
that leads him onward – a vocation
year in, year out, morning to evening
looking for something, something, something.

Nothing will stop him. Although distracted
by nest-building, eggs, high winds, high tides
and too short a life-span for him to plan
an intelligent search – still, on he goes
with his delicate legs and spillikin feet
and the wish to know what he's almost guessed.
Can't leave it alone, that stretch of sand.
Thinks himself Seurat (pointilliste)
or a molecular physicist.
Poor bird, he is obsessed!

And just because he has not yet found
what he doesn't know he is searching for
is not a sign he's off the track.
His track is the sedge, the sand, the suck
of the undertow, the line of shells.
Nor would he have it another way.
And yet – the nag – is there something else?
Something more, perhaps, or something less.
And though he examine them, day after day
the millions of grains are black, white, tan and gray.

But occasionally, when he least expects it,
in the glass of a wave a painted fish
like a work of art across his sight
reminds him of something he doesn't know
that he has been seeking his whole long life –
something that may not even exist!
Poor bird, indeed! Poor dazed creature!
Yet when his eye is sharp and sideways seeing
oh, *then* the quotidian unexceptional sand is
mixed with quartz grains, rose and amethyst.

During the day I laugh and during the night I sleep.
My favourite cooks prepare my meals,
my body cleans and repairs itself,
and all my work goes well.

I Have Not Lingered in European   Leonard Cohen
Monasteries

Here is eternity as we dream it – perfect.
Another dimension. Here the ship of state
has sprung no leaks, the captain doesn't lie.
The days are perfect and each perfect minute
extends itself forever at my wish.
Unending sunlight falls upon the steep
slope of the hillside where the children play.
And I am beautiful. I know my worth
and when I smile I show my perfect teeth.
During the day I laugh and during the night I sleep.

A dreamless, healing sleep. I waken
to everlasting Greece as white and blue
as music in my head –
an innocent music.
I had forgotten such innocence exists,
forgotten how it feels
to live with neither calendars nor clocks.
I had forgotten how to un-me myself.
Now, as I practise how and my psyche heals
my favourite cooks prepare my meals.

I am not without appetite, nor am I greedy.
My needs are as undemanding as my tastes:
spring water, olives, cucumber and figs
and a small fish on a white plate.
To lift my heart I have no wish for wine –
the sparkling air is my aperitif.
Like Emily I am inebriate.
Rude health is mine – and privilege. I bathe
in sacred waters of the river Alph.
My body cleans and repairs itself.

Poised between Earth and Heaven, here I stand
proportions perfect – arms and legs outspread
within a circle – Leonardo's man.
So do I see the giddy Cosmos. Stars
beyond stars unfold for me and shine.
My telephoto lens makes visible
time future and time past, and timeless time
receives me like its child. I am become
as intricate and simple as a cell
and all my work goes well.

The provinces of his body revolted,
The squares of his mind were empty,
Silence invaded the suburbs,
The current of his feeling failed: he became his admirers.

In Memory of W.B. Yeats   *W.H. Auden*

Rebel troops overran his palace.
A despot assumed the throne.
In his once peaceable kingdom
after the looting began
great bonfires eclipsed the moon.
The downtrodden all exulted
believing their time had come.
When his crown fell and his sceptre
and he was no longer consulted
the provinces of his body revolted.

In his perfectly tended parks
tall nettles sprang up and dockweed.
On his exhibition grounds
where merry-go-rounds had turned
and a ferris-wheel uptilted
the gypsies had broken camp.
Their rubbish alone was left.
He was a vacant lot,
he had become an exemption.
The squares of his mind were empty.

A light snow fell in summer.
His lakes were frozen over.
No forecaster had foreseen
such unseasonable weather.
Even his birds migrated.
Nothing could now disturb
the white infinity
of his radically altered syntax
the total absence of verbs.
Silence invaded the suburbs.

Only his nouns remained
and one by one they vanished.
Then when the traffic stopped
and silence invaded the towns
he became a soundless country.
We covered the many mirrors;
we covered his eyes with pennies.
His answering service broke down
and his state-of-the-art computers
the current of his feeling failed: he became his admirers.

There they were as our guests, accepted and accepting.
So we moved, and they, in a formal pattern,
Along the empty alley, into the box circle,
To look down into the drained pool.

Burnt Norton   *T.S. Eliot*

Extraordinary presences, the sunlight seeming
to light them from within, tall alabaster
amphoras with flames inside them
motionless within the grove, their shadows
like chlorophyl, like leaves, like water
slipping from a silver jug, reflecting
grasses, the long pliant stalks of willows.
And when they turned to us, their brightness spilled
over our skin and hair and, like a blessing,
there they were as our guests, accepted and accepting.

Only our golden selves went forth to greet them
that part of us which receiving blows
feels neither pain nor grief, the part that senses
joy in a higher register and moves
through a country of continuous light
shed by the one god, by the sun god, Aten –
moves as Nefertiti and her daughters
moved through their city of continuous light
in the pharaonic kingdom of Aknaten.
So we moved, and they, in a formal pattern.

Our feet barely touched the earth, and memory
erased at birth, but gradually reassembling
coalesced and formed a whole, as single birds
gathering for migration form a flock.
And some new incandescence in our heads
led us from the shadows to the sparkle
of Aten-light where we at last remembered
the arc of our lives, the distant stars we came from
and walked – O joy, O very miracle! –
along the empty alley, into the box circle.

And so to the maze with its forking paths which seen
from above, entire, was like a map –
or like a rose unfolding, a yellow rose,
opening in the unreflecting air –
the green of its leaves
the Garden before the fall,
every atom accurately aligned,
and there we walked in youthful innocence
until we came at last – new-born, royal –
to look down into the drained pool.

PLANET EARTH

It has to be spread out, the skin of this planet,
has to be ironed, the sea in its whiteness;
and the hands keep on moving,
smoothing the holy surfaces.

In Praise of Ironing   *Pablo Neruda*

It has to be loved the way a laundress loves her linens,
the way she moves her hands caressing the fine muslins
knowing their warp and woof,
like a lover coaxing, or a mother praising.
It has to be loved as if it were embroidered
with flowers and birds and two joined hearts upon it.
It has to be stretched and stroked.
It has to be celebrated.
O this great beloved world and all the creatures in it.
It has to be spread out, the skin of this planet.

The trees must be washed, and the grasses and mosses.
They have to be polished as if made of green brass.
The rivers and little streams with their hidden cresses
and pale-coloured pebbles
and their fool's gold
must be washed and starched or shined into brightness,
the sheets of lake water
smoothed with the hand
and the foam of the oceans pressed into neatness.
It has to be ironed, the sea in its whiteness

and pleated and goffered, the flower-blue sea
the protean, wine-dark, grey, green, sea
with its metres of satin and bolts of brocade.
And sky – such an O! overhead – night and day
must be burnished and rubbed
by hands that are loving
so the blue blazons forth
and the stars keep on shining
within and above
and the hands keep on moving.

It has to be made bright, the skin of this planet
till it shines in the sun like gold leaf.
Archangels then will attend to its metals
and polish the rods of its rain.
Seraphim will stop singing hosannas
to shower it with blessings and blisses and praises
and, newly in love,
we must draw it and paint it
our pencils and brushes and loving caresses
smoothing the holy surfaces.

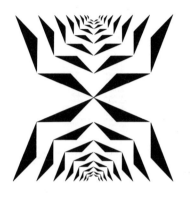

Though they go mad they shall be sane,
Though they sink through the sea they shall rise again;
Though lovers be lost love shall not;
And death shall have no dominion.

And Death Shall Have No Dominion   Dylan Thomas

Tell me the truth. How does it end?
Who will untangle their matted hair?
Shine in the dark hole of their sleep?
Though they rattle the stones in their broken brains,
in their thicket of words who will find a way,
discover a path through unmapped terrain?
When will the unpretentious air
fall like rain on the ache of their skin?
What is the price they pay for pain?

Though they go mad they shall be sane.

What is the hope for those who drown?
Pickled in brine? Stripped to the bone?
Who will they meet in deep sea lanes?
Or, when they find themselves alone,
too far up or too far down
beyond the reach of hell or heaven
how will they speak who have no tongue?
Who will they be when their bones are gone?
Bodiless, are they anyone?

Though they sink through the sea they shall rise again.

And what of the heart like an empty cup;
heart like a drum; red blood – white?
How can they twin when their love has gone?
How can they live when their love has died?
When the reins to their chariot have been cut?
What of the plot and counterplot
families devise to keep apart
Romeo from Juliet?
And what of the lovers of Camelot?

Though lovers be lost love shall not.

Love shall not. O, love shall not.
Engrave it in stone. Carve it in rock.
This is the sub-text of all art,
the wind in the wings of the Paraclete.
With the Lord of the Dance we shall form a ring
and there in love's pavilion
hand in hand we shall say Amen
and we shall dance and we shall sing
with Love, with Love for companion.

And death shall have no dominion.

ALONE

The moon is set and the Pleiades
It is midnight and time passes
Time passes
I lie alone

Sappho

Summer and the honeyed air
rises, falls – like a lover breathing.
The only sound, this slow breathing
from the high branches of the pines
in dark so dark I might be blind.
Am I blind? Perhaps my eyes
now they are no longer needed
for seeing you
have atrophied.
The moon is set and the Pleiades.

I saw them set. I saw the light
fade overhead, fade all around me.
I felt eternity enter my veins
slow drip of an intravenous needle
that drop by drop anaesthetizes
greys me, turns the night to ashes
but will not let me sleep, I wait
for words I shall not hear
caresses …
It is midnight and time passes.

Passes. 'To pass.'
What is this verb
that means 'to move
go on, progress'?
This is not movement
this is stasis.
Something has broken
turned to stone.
Meaning reverses.
Time passes

means 'does not pass'.
Time does not pass.
Is stopped.
Concluded.
Once, God was here
to mark the end
that love began.
Now darkness reigns.
And God has gone.
I lie alone.

A BAGATELLE

Rose-red, princess hibiscus, rolling her pointed Chinese petals!
Azalea and camellia, single peony
And pomegranate bloom and scarlet mallow-flower
And all the eastern, exquisite royal plants ...

Hibiscus and Salvia Flowers   *D.H. Lawrence*

What a garden I tumble into.
What a froth
and buzz of blossoms.
Sun hot and glazing leather-leaf,
sun oiling and waxing
rubbing up its metals
and there, resplendent,
attended by her oriental court officials
royally sprawling and bedecked with medals
rose-red Princess Hibiscus, rolling her pointed Chinese petals.

Enthroned and indolent in her green apparel
her sole purpose
to dazzle, to be admired,
how red her blue blood
how rose-of-China
her roseate blossoms – one-a-penny –
each a perfect kiss.
She is a shrubful of perfect kisses
awaiting only
Azalea and Camellia, single Peony

to blossom for her,
burst into bright caresses.
Peony: asiatic buttercup
with petals by Balmain – such a line!
Camellia: curiously, named for George J. Kamel,
Moravian, a Jesuit missioner;
dainty Azalea,
crossed with Azael
that blazing visitor from a higher sphere,
and Pomegranate bloom and scarlet Mallow flower.

How they adore her! Each one of them.
They are created just
for her delectation. They devise
their intricate curlings,
crimpings, for her sake.
Princess Hibiscus, in summer residence –
their yellow-stamened, once-upon-a-time Princess –
her joyous standard blowing
among the ginkgos, bamboos, flowering quince
and all the eastern exquisite royal plants.

There will only be yesterday, only the fading land,
The boats on the shore and tamarisks in the sand
Where the beautiful faces wait, and the faithful friends.
They will people your mind. You will never touch their hands.

Imagine the South   George Woodcock

Tomorrow a change of lens or soft-focus filter
will alter the past. Its edges will smudge and blur,
its embroideries and its subtleties disappear.
It will be generic, unparticular
unlike today which is bright as a name brand, clear
and familiar as the palm of your hand.
And though you may squint and shade your eyes and peer
back through time, mists will obscure the scene.
Whatever you long for has been left behind.
There will only be yesterday, only the fading land.

And memory, trickster figure, will let you down –
a fiction writer offering alternative versions
of what you had once imagined written in stone:
the immutable facts of your life. But now you question
which of them are true, and truth itself
that once appeared an end to be sought and found
becomes elusive, seems to assume disguises;
is finally and, heart-breakingly, diminished
to a dim discoloured shot of lowtide and
the boats on the shore and tamarisks in the sand.

And as for the people you loved, even their names
will escape you. Did you not mean what you said
when you said, I will love you forever? You did.
Though it's hard to remember when now you can barely recall
the lift of the chin or the quizzical tilt of the head
that filled you with wonder, nor how you counted the seconds
that felt like hours, for a glimpse … but you know the rest –
any more than your eye can recapture the angle of light
as it fell on the valleys and hills of those distant lands
where the beautiful faces wait, and the faithful friends.

They will wait and wait forever –
become like figures from dreams, or phantom limbs.
How beautiful they are, how blossoming
in your imagination. Trees in spring.
And the pain of their absence, harder to bear than death,
is with you wherever you go – a secret wound
that aches in the night, awakens you from sleep
and makes you a child again, a lonely child.
And so they will haunt you, those half-remembered friends.
They will people your mind. You will never touch their hands.

For whom do you live? Can it be yourself?
For whom then? Not for this unlovely world,
Not for the rotting waters of mischance,
Nor for the tall, eventual catafalque.

The Vow   *Robert Graves*

Tell me every detail of your day –
when do you wake and sleep, what eat and drink?
How spend the interval from dawn to dark –
what do you work at, read, what do you think?
Whom do you love and how much? – Measure it
and answer me, or leastwise, answer half.
These are not idle questions, they provide
the spindle around which new-spinning wool
winds as it dreams its future warp and woof.
For whom do you live? Can it be yourself?

No. Your answers prove it – they are tinged
with another pigment, glow with light
from a strange sun, *contre-jour*, back-lit –
a light that would have taxed all Monet's skills
and, fading, left him knowing he had failed.
Your answers, though transparent, issue veiled
hermetic, deeply hidden, you speak in code.
A huge enigma hides in your replies.
Not live for the self – first love, unparalleled?
For whom then? 'Not for this unlovely world,

'world we have made unlovely, world we have used,
as if it were ours to tamper with, ours to destroy
and so we have destroyed it, like a child
taking his father's watch apart, or worse, a fly –
removing its prismed, fragile wings.
Destroyed it not for myrrh nor frankincense,
but gold, O Midas. We have sacked for gold.
Nor do I live for what it could have been
had we been otherwise. Not for providence,
not for the rotting waters of mischance,

'but love, only for love, the love that is
so focussed on its object that I die
utterly, a candle in the sun,
a drop of water in the sea.
I do not live for heaven's promises
in fear of purgatory or hell's deadlock
but for that beam of love which clothes us in
ephemeral garment's coronation cloth –
not wealth, not jewels, not sovereignty, not silk
nor for the tall, eventual catafalque.'

THE END

Not every man knows what he shall sing at the end,
Watching the pier as the ship sails away, or what it will seem like
When he's held by the sea's roar, motionless, there at the end,
Or what he shall hope for once it is clear that he'll never go back.

The End   Mark Strand

In the story, you come at last to a high wall.
Some who have scaled it say they were stricken blind
yet lacked a blind man's skills – white cane, dark glasses.
One girl I know clambered up and gazing over
saw the familiar universe reversed
as in a looking glass. But when that world
beckoned to her complicitously, she turned
from its mirror image as if burned –
wordless, without music, without sound.
Not every man knows what he shall sing at the end.

And one, composed of light, came back he said
to tell me it was not *not* everlasting there
as once he had assumed, that I was right.
Was he not proof? 'Touch me,' he said. I touched
and he was flesh, blood, hair – even as before.
It was the purest heartbreak.
'Tell me …' I said. Bemused, he shook his head.
'It's personal. When your turn comes you'll know.
Till then you cannot guess what you will think
watching the pier as the ship sails away, or what it will seem like,

'nor can I possibly tell you.' His voice was fading
and beneath the palms of my hands he suddenly vanished
as if he had never been – except for two things:
in the darkness I could see, and I was staring
at my fingers where they had touched him, staring
at my mouth, new, where he had kissed it; and
it was clear to me now there was nothing to fear
and no reason for anyone, here or anywhere
to suppose he will be drowned
when he's held by the sea's roar, motionless, there at the end.

For he belongs to the sea – we all do. We are part of its swell.
And only the shoreline grounds us. Yet we stand
hands tied, deluded, seemingly earthbound
imagining we belong to the land
which is only a way-station, after all.
We are the sea's, and as such we are at its beck.
We are the water within the wave and the wave's form.
And little will man – or woman, come to that –
know what he shall dream when drawn by the sea's wrack
or what he shall hope for once it is clear that he'll never go back.

ACKNOWLEDGEMENTS

'Hologram', 'Presences', 'Love's Pavilion' and 'Planet Earth'
were published in *The Malahat Review*; 'The Gold Sun', 'Poor
Bird', 'In Memoriam' and 'Autumn' in *Prairie Schooner*; and 'A
Bagatelle', 'The Answer' and 'The End' in *Exile*. 'Planet Earth'
also appeared in *Living at the End of the Second Millennium*;
Clear-Cut Words: Writers for Clayoquot; and *Clayoquot Diary*.
'Presences' and 'Planet Earth' also appeared in *Windhorse
Reader: Choice Poems of '93*.

The acknowledgements would not be complete without
thanks to Jan Zwicky whose accurate eye and musical ear
were invaluable.

P.K. Page is the author of over a dozen books of poetry, fiction, and non-fiction, and has been honoured with numerous awards, including the Governor General's Award for poetry. Her paintings have been exhibited internationally and she is represented in the permanent collections of The National Gallery of Canada, the Art Gallery of Ontario, and many other museums. Having travelled widely for much of her life, she now makes her home in Victoria.